The Divergence of Price Action & Trend Reversal

Hidden Strategy…

By

Er. SUDHIR KUMAR SAHU

Dedicated to
My parents, my family, my well
wishers & my departed brother
Dr. Srimanta.

ACKNOWLEDGEMENTS

The support & encouragement of my family, friends & well wishers create enthusiasm to achieve something in life. Several persons are associated to create something, without which such type of efforts would not be possible. I would like to thanks my parents, whose love & guidance are always with me. They brought me to this world & continuously blessed me to make me an able person in the society. Thanks to my wife for supporting me. The cover page, the main attraction of this book is designed by my eldest daughter Samanwita. My youngest daughter Samapika, always inspired me, which cannot be denied. Many others who have helped me, both professionally & personally in writing this book also need acknowledgement. I am thankful to google for providing treasure of information to write this book. Last but not the least, I thank God for his enormous blessings.

SUDHIR

CONTENTS

PREFACE

When two related components move in the same direction, it is concluded as convergence. When they move in the opposite direction, it is divergence. Thus, two things or actions are moving apart in opposite directions. Divergence is one powerful trading concept, which determines the trend direction and contemplates an effective trading signal.

Traders generally use divergence for two purposes; assessing the price action & trend reversal. In technical analysis, divergence is an indicator of positive or negative price action. For positive or bullish divergence, the price action moves lower lows and the indicator that tracks this action indicates higher lows. Conversely, for negative or bearish divergence, the price action moves higher highs and the indicator that tracks this action indicates lower highs. The essence of this book has been simplified as much as possible to inculcate and accommodate the most novice traders &

1

investors of the stock market. This book is written only for educational purposes. The profit & loss is trader's responsibility.

INTRODUCTION

Due to some positive or negative news flow like political turmoil, war, pandemic, election etc., there could be high demand & supply for a particular stock. During emergence of such big news, there is high volatility in the market. Demand & Supply, the most fundamental concepts of economics are the two driving forces in stock market. Sentiment drives demand & supply, consequently stock price. Demand is the quantity, that the consumers want to buy at different prices. Supply is the quantity, that the producers want to sold into the market. When price of the goods increase, there is demand for the product and consequently price of the product increases. Proper balance must be maintained to achieve equilibrium so as both consumers & producers are benefitted. The law of demand & supply is attributed to economic theory propounded by Adam Smith in 1776. The law of demand & supply contemplates, if some product has high demand & low supply, the price will be more. At the variance with, if there is low demand & high supply, the price will be less.

When demand exceeds supply, price tends to rise and when supply exceeds demand, price falls. When number of buyers exceed number of sellers, the demand increases and price goes up. When number of sellers exceed number of buyers, the supply increases and price goes down. The price action contemplates the fight between bulls & bears, the trend goes in favour of the stronger participant.

Due to concentration of demand at Support level, the stock price unable to penetrate below and repeatedly bounce back from that level. Likewise, due to concentration of supply at Resistance level, the stock price unable to penetrate above and repeatedly bounce back from that level. When a support level breaches, the stock price moves downward. When a resistance level breaches, the stock price moves upward. The breaching of support level is called breakdown and breaching of resistance level is called breakout. Breaching of established level may be dealt carefully. Confirmation must be followed before adopting breakout/breakdown strategy.

PRICE ACTION & MOMENTUM

Price action is simply the analysis of share price movement in the stock market without using any indicators. The direction & magnitude of price action depends upon the trend strength or price momentum. Trends are composed of series of price swings, either up, down or range bound. The price action is characterized by swing highs & lows. As ascertained, uptrend is characterized by series of higher highs & higher lows. Downtrend is characterized by series of lower highs & lower lows. The corresponding slope when steep exhibits strong price action and when it is shallow, exhibits weak price action.

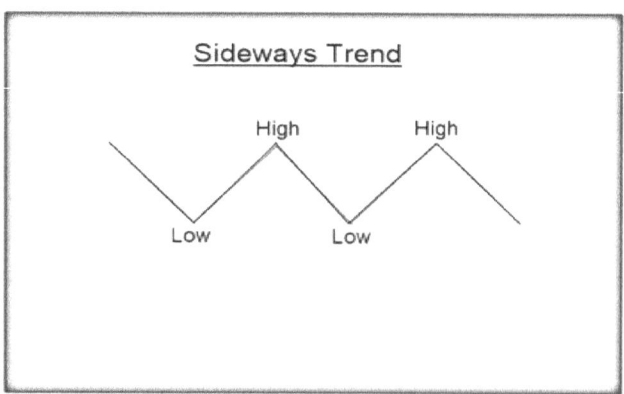

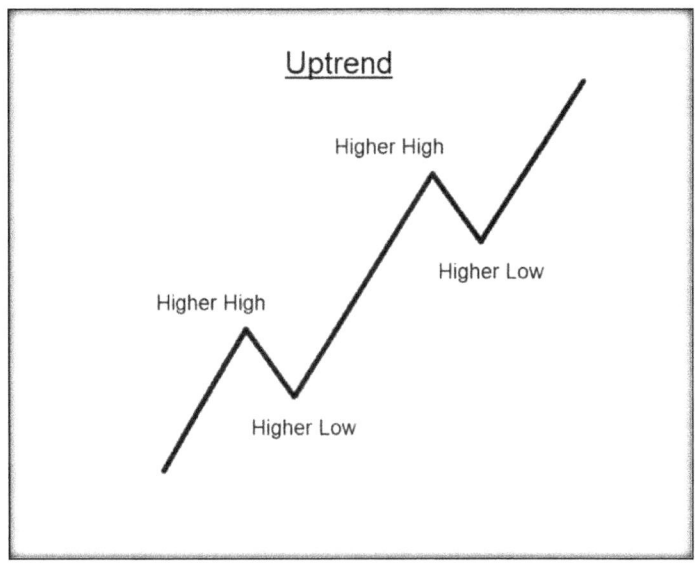

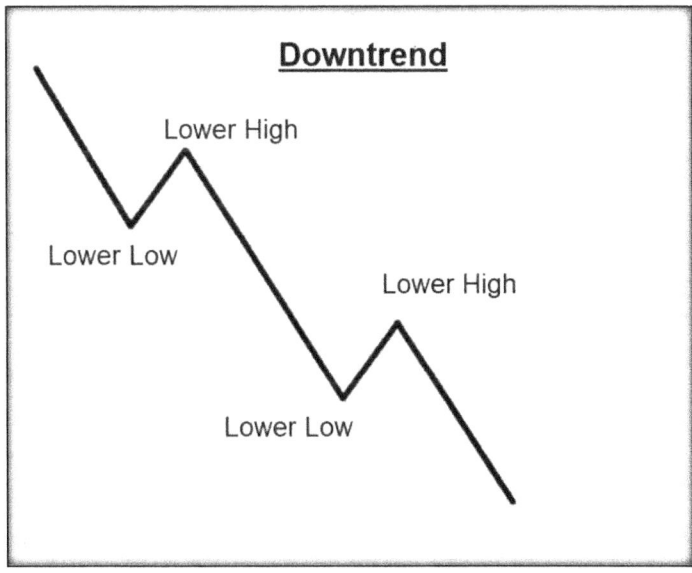

Traders or investors usually buy in uptrend and sell in downtrend. They refrain from trading during sideways trend.

The price action depicted on a chart at any given time frame represents the collective emotions of market participants. In uptrend, stock prices are moving up and implied, buyers are in control. In downtrend, stock prices are moving down and implied, sellers are in control. In a range bound market, there is consensus between the bulls & the bears. In price action trading, the only virtuous contributor of information is nothing but the price action and its movements. If price action advances in positive slope, it inculcate that investors are buying. Conversely, if price action advances in negative slope, it inculcate that investors are selling.

Price action traders contemplate that, technical indicators may sometimes lag behind price action movement and may not always provide error free indication. Usually, it is seen that, most indicators evaluate their outputs basing on closing prices. Thus, they give signals after stock price has advances or declines and perfect entry signals never be obtained. Thus, it is considered as lagging indicator.

Each & every single trading indicator of stock market is derived from the price action. The most commonly used price action indicator is the study of price bars or candlesticks. Candlesticks are graphical representation of price actions that contemplate the trend, open, close, high & low price of a stock, index or financial assets.

It is a matter of choice, basing on trading style to use standalone price action strategy or using technical indicator. The skill of a veteran trader lies in their ability to implement the precise strategy for price action. Usually, best trading strategy is obtained when combined with both trading indicators as well as price action. Technical analysis tools like RSI, MACD &

Stochastics etc. are calculated from price action and used in conjunction to predict future price action.

Price action of a stock or index is infused with global news and other sentiments of market participants, thus, everything is discounted in the price action chart. Experienced traders evaluate the price action itself without considering the lagging indicators.

For price action trading, the candlestick chart is most suitably used and considered the pre-eminent chart used. All profits & losses in stock market are based on price action. There are two important factors to be considered while analyzing price action. One is price and another is volume. Trading volume identify momentum in a price action and confirm the direction of trend. You must watch for divergence between price direction & volume. For instance, if the market makes new highs while volume falls short of the previous high, it implies the market is getting weaker.

The Correlation between Price & Volume as noted below:

Sl. No.	Price	Volume	Interpretation
1	Increasing	Increasing	Strong Buying Pressure
2	Increasing	Decreasing	Weakly Bullish
3	Decreasing	Increasing	Strong Selling Pressure
4	Decreasing	Decreasing	Weakly Bearish

Technical analyst utilizes sophisticated calculations to predict future price movements. Conversely, price action strategy solely relies on the price movements of a security within the trading timeframe.

TRENDS & TRENDLINES

In stock market trading & investing, the first and foremost step is to identify the trend. Trend is the overall direction of price movement of stock or index in stock market, either up or down. There are three types of trends depicted in the stock market, namely uptrend, downtrend & sideways trend. Uptrend is gradual increase of price or value of something; characterized by series of higher highs (peaks) & higher lows (troughs). Downtrend is gradual decrease of price or value of something; characterized by series of Lower highs (peaks) & Lower lows (troughs).

In general, two consecutive higher highs & higher lows considered as uptrend and two consecutive lower highs & lower lows considered as downtrend. Precisely, market movements happen in the form of trends. As it is described earlier, the trend is the friend of traders or investors. As such, if you trade with the trend, there will be profit and if you trade against the

12

trend, there will be loss. If you swim across the tide, you will fail. Most traders trade in the direction of the trend. Traders who trade opposite of the trend are nomenclated as contrarian investors.

When, Stock trend is stronger than market trend in uptrend, buying opportunity is found and when stock trend is weaker than market trend in downtrend, selling opportunity is found in that stock. If stock trend & market trend contradicts, then follow the stock trend. If two timeframes contradict and give opposite signal, trend may be confirmed with higher time frame chart.

Time Frames for Different types of Trades:

Sl. No.	Type of Trade	Larger Time frame	Medium time frame	Smaller time frame
1	Long Term	Weekly	Daily	4 Hours
2	Medium Term	One Day	4 Hours	1 Hour
3	Intraday	One Hour	15 Minutes	5 Minutes

In stock market, trend line is a boundary for the price action and movement of a security. A trend line starts at the beginning of a trend and culminates at the end. It is visual representation of Support & Resistance in any timeframe. Trend line is drawn over swing highs or under swing lows to interpret the prevailing direction of stock price. Usually, two or more swing points are considered to draw a trend line. The more points considered to draw the trend line, the more cogency represented by the trend line. Drawing trend lines help the traders to take rational trading decisions based on what is prevalent in the stock market. The trend lines become stronger, if more times the price action is rebounded from the support or resistance. Trend Lines usually moves with the price trend for which it is referred to as dynamic support & resistance level.

The uptrend line has a positive slope and is formed by connecting at least three low points. The successive lows must be higher than the previous lows.

The ascending trend line is formed when the low points are connected. The uptrend line connecting higher lows acts as a support of the price action. The downtrend line has a negative slope and is formed by connecting at least three high points. The successive highs must be lower than the previous highs. The descending trend line is formed when the high points are connected. The down trend line connecting lower highs acts as a resistance of the price action.

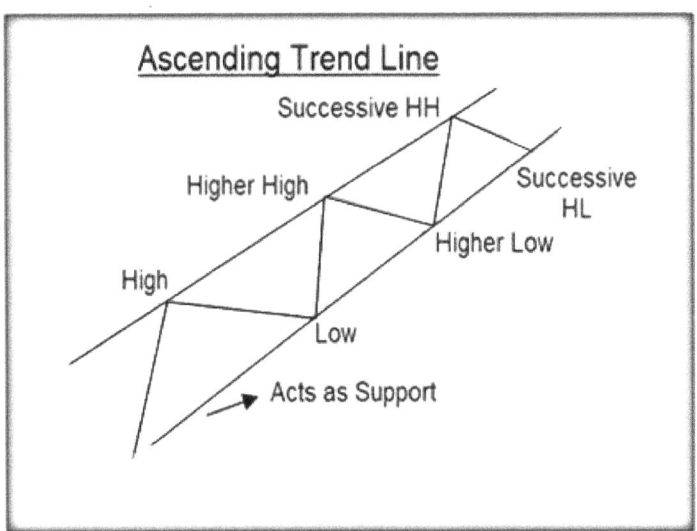

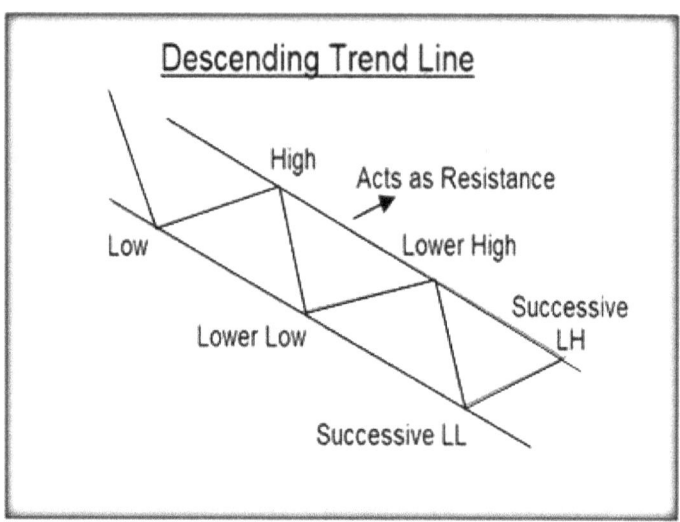

The ascending trend line having positive slope acts as support to price action indicates, demand is increasing. In such case, the number of buyers exceed the number of sellers. The descending trend line having negative slope acts as resistance to price action indicates supply is increasing. In such case, the number of sellers exceed the number of buyers.

If the price action breaks the trend lines, it may happens that the stock price will move in the direction of breakout or breakdown. If the price action in uptrend, breaches the trend line on the upside, there is possibility of trend continuation. The traders & investors may initiate new long position or add more to the existing position. If the price action in uptrend, breaches the trend line on the downside, there is possibility of trend reversal. The trader or investor may opt to close the existing position or short sell.

Trend lines may be drawn on any timeframe to suit the trading requirement. Trend lines drawn on smaller timeframes tend to break very often. This is due to the fact that, less quantity is being traded in smaller timeframe as compared to trend lines drawn on a larger timeframe. More the number of stocks traded, the stronger is the trend line.

Trend lines are also used to find reversals. Since the uptrend is characterized by higher lows, a trend line can be drawn along those higher low points. When price action drops below that trend line, it indicates a trend reversal in downside. Likewise, the downtrend is characterized by lower highs, a trend line can be drawn along those lower high points. When price action moves above that trend line, it indicates a trend reversal in upside.

Trend Lines depict the current trend irrespective of different opinions & predictions. Huge losses may happen when some trader opt to stay on the wrong side of the trend and failed to place the stop loss. The small loss from the beginning turns around in to a gigantic loss. Praying almighty and hoping the trade to turn around leads to disaster. Thus, make trade accordingly and stay with the trend.

PULLBACK, CORRECTION & REVERSAL

The Bulls & Bears are two entities of irrational stock market, which exhibit strong emotions in opposite directions. The Bull creates positive emotion & the Bear creates negative emotion. They fight among each other to stay at the top of the Sea Saw mechanism. When the Bull dominates, the market goes up; when the Bear dominates, the market goes down. The market never advances or declines in straight line; rather goes up & down in zigzag manner and create different price patterns.

It is also due to some positive or negative news flow, there could be high demand & supply for a particular stock. Whether it is more supply than demand or more demand than supply, it is the difference that creates price momentum. Stock prices at any given time do not necessarily represent the underlying value of the stock; they are driven up & down by emotions of market participants. Stock market traders make decisions based on psychological factors, including emotions.

Pullback, Retracement, Correction & Reversal are a way of life in the financial markets. Pullback, Retracement & Correction are temporary in nature, consequently short term movement of price action in opposite direction to the main trend. A correction will be temporary price increase in bearish trend and price decrease in bullish trend. Very often traders & investors profit book their stocks causing the stock price to experience pull back or retracement in share price. Thus, the theory of retracement implies to the correction of prevailing price movement. The price action will be depicted by indecisive candles like doji & spinning top. Reversal candles are depicted by different pattern like double top & bottom, triple top & bottom, Head & shoulder, Inverse Head & Shoulder etc. and many more.

Retracements are temporary price reversals due to profit taking by retail traders or investors within a larger trend. Retracements provide opportunity to new investors for an entry point at low level for potential future profit and identifying protective stop level to minimize risk. Retracement, pullback & correction are words, very often used interchangeably. The most popular retracement assessment tool might be Fibonacci retracement, which the traders use to identify strategic levels for stock trading. The most commonly used Fibonacci retracement levels are at 23.6%, 38.2%, 50%, 61.8%, 78.6%. The Fibonacci sequence is 0, 1, 1, 2, 3, 5, 8, 13, 21, 34, 55, 89 and so on. Each new number in the sequence is the sum of the two previous numbers. Fibonacci retracement levels were named after Italian mathematician Leonardo Pisano Bigollo, popularly known as Leonardo Fibonacci. The retracements are a short trend in itself but with a direction opposite to the main trend.

Stock price movement that retraces in opposite direction from earlier movement due to adverse news, either fully or partly is termed as correction. Correction is temporary price decline. Corrections offer opportunity to enter a stock at a lower level. In spite of negative news if the stock did not retraces, it is a sign of strength. Conversely, in spite of positive news if the stock did not rise; it is a sign of weakness.

On the other side, Reversals are sudden & long term retracement, might be due to institutional selling of stocks in large block or financial degradation of company fundamentals. As such, the price pattern is likely to continue in that reversal direction for an extended period.

Uptrend is very often characterized by a sequence of higher highs & higher lows. Similarly, downtrend is characterized by a sequence of lower highs & lower lows. The trend is said to be reverse when the sequence is broken. When a trend line is broken, the market may either reverse the trend, continue in the same direction with less momentum or just time pass in sideways or range bound market.

Since uptrend line is drawn through higher low points, when an up trending trend line is broken, the trend may continue either upward with less pace or reverse downward or go sideways. The upward trend line is said to be the area of support. Similarly, down trend line is drawn through lower high points. When a down trending trend line is broken, the trend may continue either downward with less pace or reverse upward or go sideways. The downward trend line is said to be the area of resistance.

Ralph Nelson Elliot of America developed wave theory in 1930, which postulates financial markets have characteristic movements that repeat in a cyclical fashion. He called these movements as "waves" due to the presence of peaks & troughs in up & down fashion. Elliot found that, when a trend is in progress, it has

23

typically three large price moves called impulse waves in the direction of main trend and two corrections called as corrective waves opposite to the main trend. The impulse waves & corrective waves are constituted with several smaller waves trending in the corresponding directions. Elliot wave 'C' is the end of the correction, before the prior trend resumes. Elliot Wave theory is a technical analysis of price pattern related to changes in Investor's sentiment & psychology. Thus, Elliot Wave principle help investors to decide Entry, Exit & Profit booking target. Elliot Wave theory in standalone does not work accurately, hence, may be used with other indicators.

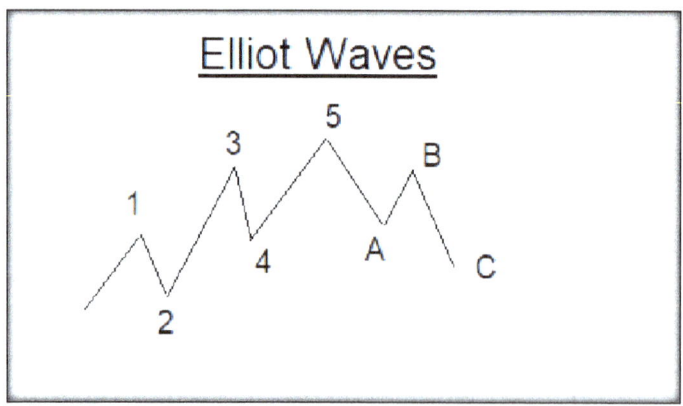

The reversal might be upside or downside. In uptrend, the reversal would be to the downside. In downtrend, the reversal would be to the upside.

THE CONCEPT OF DIVERGENCE

Divergence is a scenario, when price action & indicator contradicts each others, i.e., moves in opposite direction. Divergence signals that, the current price trend is weakening and a trend reversal is ensuing. However, divergence does not always lead to trend reversal; might be sideways consolidation after a divergence. Divergence just signals a loss of momentum, but does not necessarily signal a complete trend reversal. Basically, a divergence exists when technical indicator does not agree with price action. For divergence to exist, the slope line connecting the indicators' top or bottom differs from that of price action. When the indicator & price action are out of sync, something hidden is happening on the chart, require special attention. There is positive & negative divergence.

Price action always gives the most up to date information. Ideally, traders want confirmation to enter in to a trade. Price action and indicator usually move in the same direction. Thus, while in trade, traders want their indicators to signal in sync with the price action and stock price move likely to be continued. But due to divergence, price action and indicator does not move in the same direction and consequently follow the indicator. In case of bullish divergence, stock price likely to move upward inspite of bearish sentiment prevailing. In case of bearish divergence, stock price likely to move down ward inspite of bullish sentiment prevailing.

Generally, there are two types of indicators; leading & lagging indicators. Leading indicators predict future direction, while lagging indicators confirm the past price movement. RSI & Stochastics are popular leading indicator, while MACD is popular lagging indicator. These indicators are used to spot divergences.

RSI Divergence:- The Relative Strength Index is an oscillator that is used to assess the direction of market momentum. RSI indicator ranges between 0 and 100. RSI below 30 is considered oversold and above 70 is overbought. Sometimes, the oversold & overbought levels are set at 20 & 80 instead of 30 & 70 or customized to any value. The RSI is calculated by averaging the losses & profits over the previous 14 period. If you have bought stock and RSI crosses above 70, exit from the trade and book profit. If you have sold stock and RSI crosses below 30, exit from the trade and book profit.

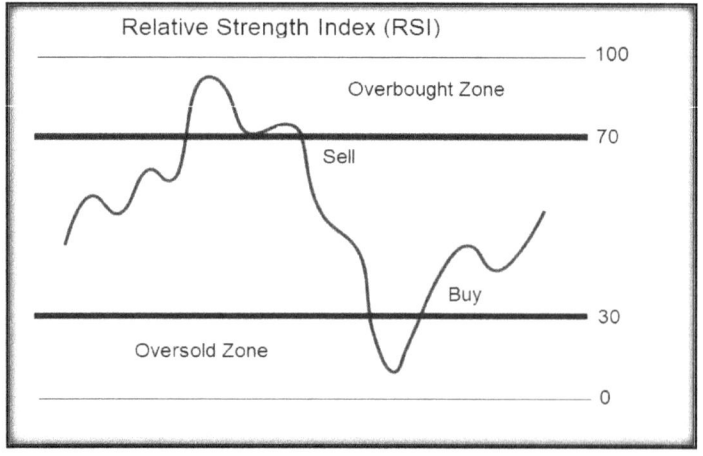

Stock price in uptrend increases with succeeding higher highs. Thus, closing prices are likely to be higher than its opening prices on each advances of price action. RSI indicator also increases as well in uptrend. Conversely, Stock price in down trend decreases with succeeding lower lows. Thus, closing prices are likely to be lower than its opening prices on each advances of price action. RSI indicator also decreases as well in down trend.

Relative Strength Index (RSI) analyzes closing prices of stocks and compare them with the opening prices over a specific period of time to depict the trend of price action. The price action & indicator often moves in sync; but price action does not move in straight line. Before making trend change, the price action slows down which can be visualized through the indicator. The exhaustion of trend & its upcoming reversal is hidden in the indicator. The price action alone does not indicate reversal signal beforehand.

But, using indicator, the exhaustion & trend reversal can be ascertained earlier. Such early signal gives the trader a better entry point for the trade.

RSI value above 70 marks overbought condition and generates sell signal. RSI value below 30 marks oversold condition and generates buy signal. In overbought condition, it is advisable to close long position and initiate short position. In oversold condition, it is advisable to close short position and initiate long position. This may not happen always, hence, to confirm & double confirm with other indicators.

When RSI indicator disagree with the price action, it indicate divergence and price action likely to change. Upon emergence of divergence, either bullish or bearish, the price action changes accordingly. However, it does not necessarily stand for trend reversal to follow.

Bullish divergence is characterized by RSI indicator making higher lows and price action making lower lows. The traders initiate long positions under such circumstances. Bearish divergence is characterized by RSI indicator making lower highs and price action making higher highs. The traders initiate short positions under such circumstances. Bullish divergence in RSI is associated with oversold condition and bearish divergence in RSI is associated with overbought condition.

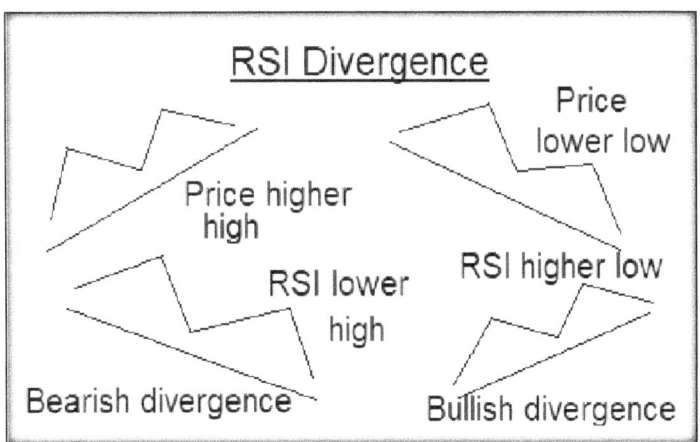

Every indicator has different settings & time periods to provide most appropriate trading signals. RSI also be applied to all timeframes & customized time period depending upon required trading strategy. For RSI intraday trading, standard setting is 14 period and 1 hour timeframe.

Stochastic Divergence:- The Stochastic is an oscillator that is used to measure stock price momentum to determine stock trend and predict reversal. Stochastic indicator ranges between 0 and 100. Value below 20 oversold and above 80 is overbought. Stochastic oscillator was developed by George Lane in 1950. Stochastic indicator works on the principle that, change in stock price is preceded by change in momentum.

A bullish divergence occurs when the stock price makes lower lows and the Stochastic Oscillator forms higher lows. When bullish divergence happens, the stock price may shift upwards, and indicates potential strength. A bearish divergence forms when the stock price makes higher highs and the Stochastic Oscillator forms lower highs. When bearish divergence happens, the stock price may shift down wards, and indicates potential weakness.

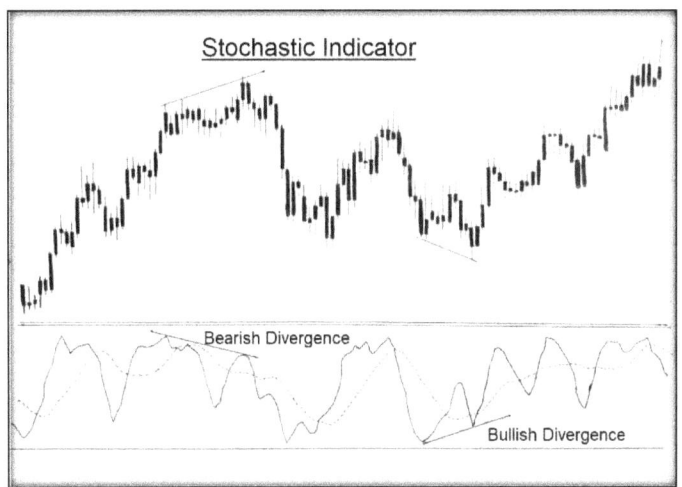

MACD Divergence:- Moving Average Convergence Divergence or MACD is one technical indicator, which tells the overall market sentiment in short to medium term. MACD indicator composed of MACD line, Signal line, Zero line & Histogram bar. The crossover of the MACD line & Signal line gives trading signals. If MACD line (Blue or Green line) crosses over Signal line (Red or black line) from bottom to top, it indicates positive cross over and bullish trend. The positive cross over below centre line indicates weak buy signal & above centerline indicates strong buy signal. When positive cross over happens below centre line & on the way crosses above centre line also indicates strong buy signal.

If MACD line (Blue or Green line) crosses below Signal line (Red or black line) from top to bottom, it indicates negative cross over and bearish trend. The negative cross over above centre line indicates weak sell signal & below centerline indicates strong sell signal. When negative cross over happens above centre line & on the way crosses below centre line also indicates strong sell signal.

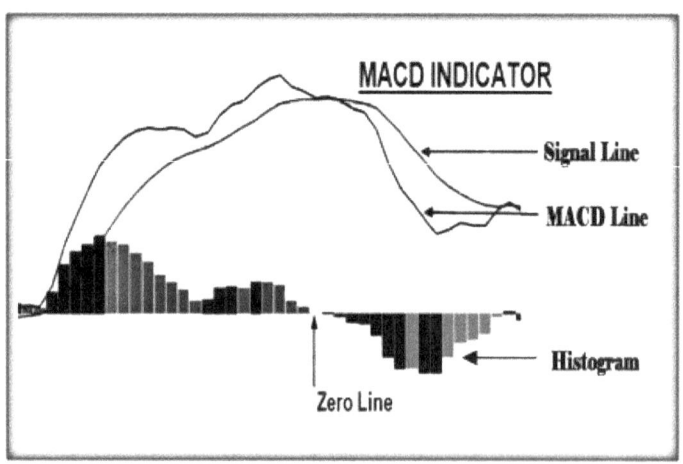

When MACD indicator contradicts with price action, divergence occurs. There are two types of divergences, namely, Bullish & Bearish. The Bullish divergence is characterized by stock prices making lower lows and MACD indicator making higher lows. MACD bullish divergence indicates buy signal. The Bearish divergence is characterized by stock prices making higher highs and MACD indicator making lower highs. MACD bearish divergence indicates sell signal.

MACD Histogram Divergence:- MACD Histogram is the difference between MACD line & Signal line. The Histogram fluctuates above or below Zero line. The histogram is positive when the MACD line is above the signal line and negative when the MACD line is below the signal line. The colour of the Histogram does not matter, however, increasing Histogram indicates trend continuation and decreasing Histogram indicates trend reversal. When the market price is moving strongly in one direction, the histogram will increase in height, and when the histogram shrinks, it shows that market is moving slower. Thus, increase in histogram bar is an indication of good strength. If histogram becoming smaller, a very big move is coming up shortly. If MACD Histogram increases above zero line or decreases below zero line indicates bullish trend. If MACD Histogram increases below zero line or decreases above zero line, it indicates bearish trend. MACD above zero line for a considerable period of time indicates uptrend and below zero line indicates down trend. Thus, when MACD stays above zero line, buying opportunity is found and MACD below zero line generates sell signal.

MACD Histogram also produces two types of divergence. Bullish & Bearish divergence. Bullish divergence of MACD Histogram occurs when stock price & MACD line advances with successive lower lows and MACD Histogram makes successive higher lows. Bearish divergence of MACD Histogram occurs when stock price & MACD line advances with successive higher highs and MACD Histogram makes successive lower highs.

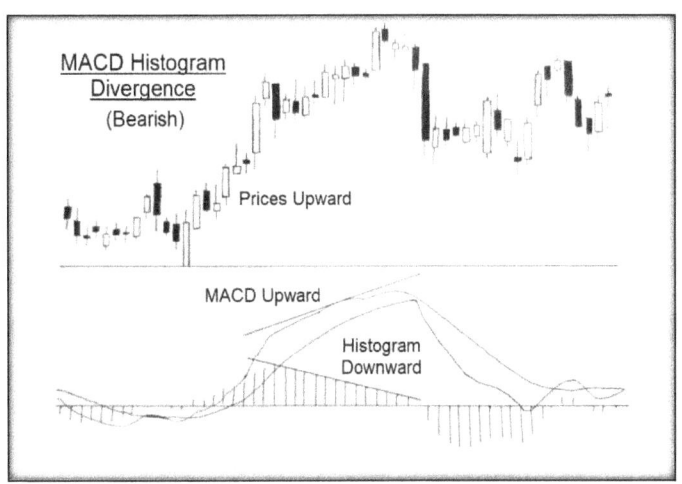

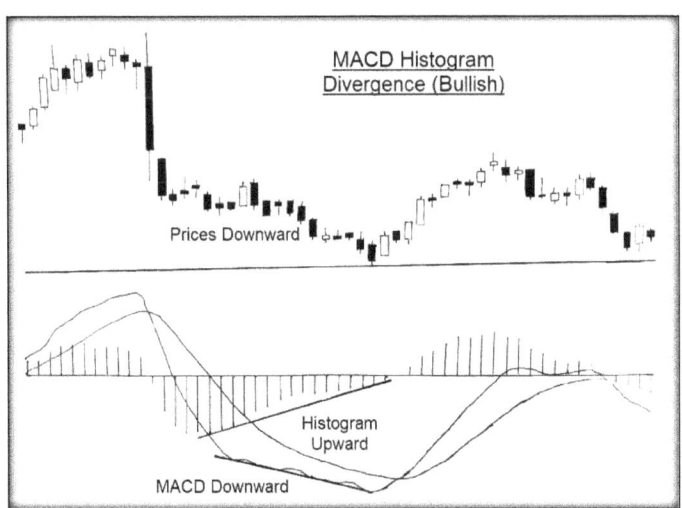

MACD histogram shows not only who have control over the market, but also provide the magnitude of strength for future price action.

The present histogram depicts the price action of the security. When current bar of the Histogram is higher than the previous bar, the slope is positive i.e., upward. Such histogram signifies that, bulls are in control and the traders can go long. When current bar of the Histogram is lower than the previous bar, the slope is negative i.e., downward. Such histogram signifies that, bears are in control and the traders can go short.

Volume Divergence:- Volume divergence occurs, when price action is not supported by trading volume. When price action makes higher high, it is uptrend. Volume must be in increasing trend. If volume makes lower high, the uptrend is not supported by volume. It is divergence. Conversely, when price action makes lower high, it is down trend. In such case volume also supposed to be increased. But, if volumes

makes lower high, the down trend is not supported by

volume. Thus trend reversal is anticipated.

Volume Price Divergence:

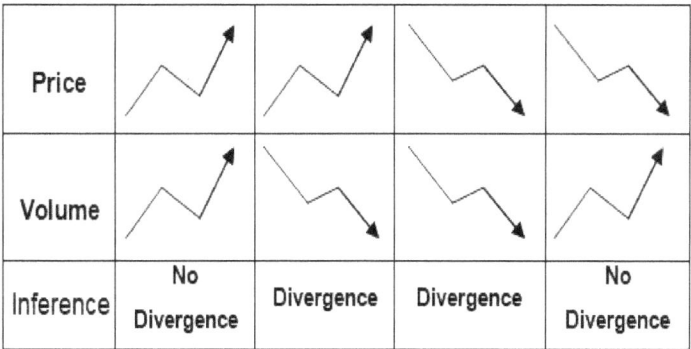

Price				
Volume				
Inference	No Divergence	Divergence	Divergence	No Divergence

Divergence of volume warns that, current trend

of price action is likely to be exhausted and somewhere

the price action is ready to take u-turn.

BULLISH REVERSAL PATTERNS

For Bullish Divergence, traders would analyze at the lows on the indicator & price action. If the price exhibits lower lows but the indicator exhibits higher lows, it is construed as bullish divergence. This may indicate rising momentum with increased buying pressure after appearance of divergence. Stock prices move ahead with higher highs & higher lows in uptrend and lower highs & lower lows in down trend.

In down trend, when price pattern appeared as double bottom, triple bottom, inverted head & shoulder and special candle like hammer, inverted hammer, morning star etc., the price action might take reversal and move upside. These are called as bullish reversal pattern. Some of the bullish reversal patterns are as depicted below.

Double Bottom:- A double bottom is a price pattern in stock chart, resembling the English letter 'W' & signal for a bullish price movement. A long position is initiated with upside breakout. Stop Loss is placed just below the breakout point or at the second bottom (B2) of the pattern. The profit target would be the height of the pattern.

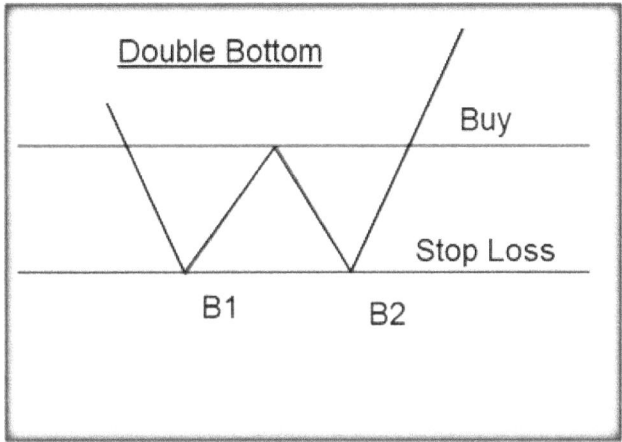

Triple Bottom:- The triple bottom is a bullish reversal pattern that occurs at the end of a downtrend. The triple bottom consists of the three consecutive lows at the same or near same level. Stop Loss is placed just below the breakout point or at the 3rd bottom (B3) of the pattern. The profit target would be the height of the pattern.

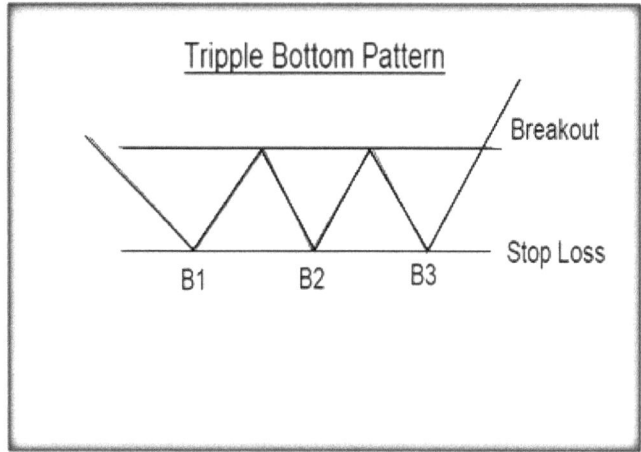

Inverted Head & Shoulder:- Inverse Head & Shoulder is a bullish reversal chart pattern which is formed during downtrend. It is the reverse of Head & Shoulder pattern. The most common entry point is when the price moves above the neckline. The height of the pattern from the breakout price will be the profit target. Stop Loss will be placed below the neck line at the peak of the right shoulder.

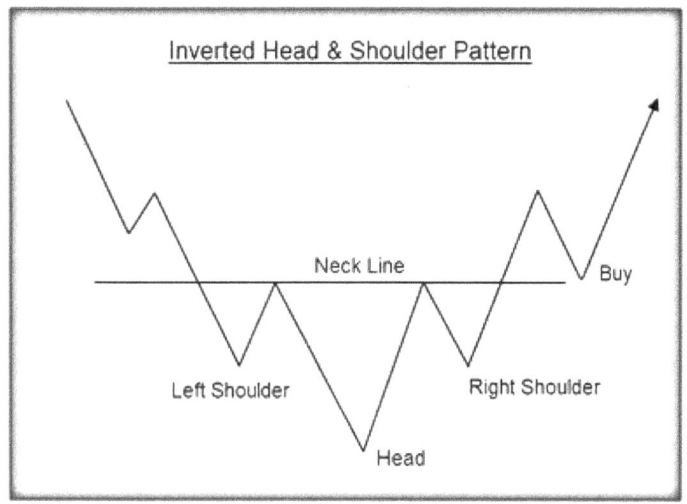

Hammer:- A small green or red candle body having long lower shadow with or without small upper shadow found during a downtrend is called Hammer. Both Hammer & Hanging Man looks exactly same in appearance; but the former forms in a downtrend and the later forms in an uptrend. Irrespective of the colour of the body, hammer indicates a bullish signal. Green hammer is more bullish than a Red hammer. With the formation of Hammer, the Bulls finally take the control & start buying. Thus, hammer is a bullish reversal pattern. The traders can initiate a bullish option strategy like buying of Calls, selling of Puts, Buying Covered Call, Bull Call Spread, Bull Put Spread etc. upon confirmation of Hammer signal with rising volume. Prices should cross above the top of the Hammer's body for confirmation. The bottom of the Hammer is a good support line and stop loss may be placed at or just below the bottom line. The structure of a hammer looks as below.

Inverted Hammer:- A small green or red candle body having long upper shadow with little or no lower shadow; found during a downtrend. Irrespective of the colour of the body, Inverted hammer indicates a bullish reversal signal. Green body is more bullish than a Red body. With the formation of Inverted Hammer, the bulls finally take the control & start buying. Hammer & Inverted Hammer is similar in nature, but Inverted Hammer is upside in appearance. Inverted Hammer & Shooting Star looks exactly the same, but the former being found in downtrend and the later being found in an uptrend. The bottom of the body of the Inverted Hammer is a good support line and stop loss may be placed at or just below the bottom line. You can initiate a bullish option strategy upon confirmation of Inverted Hammer signal with rising volume. In normal candlestick pattern, inverted hammer candle is either green or red.

The emergence of Inverted Hammer candle in the downtrend gives bullish reversal signal and the stock price moves upward. The traders who have sold into a market might consider this as a signal to start looking to exit their respective short trades and find opportunity to buy.

Morning Star:- Morning Star pattern is a combination of 3 candles. In a down trend, When a large red candle followed by Doji and a smaller green candle found in a downtrend, a morning star signal is formed. The 1st candle is red, the 2nd candle formed gap down or normal and may be of any colour, but either doji or spinning top and the 3rd candle formed gap up or normal and green in colour. Morning Star indicates something good coming ahead i.e., the stock price/index will increase. As soon as the Morning Star pattern is confirmed, there is possibility of trend reversal. The size of the 3rd candle with respect to 1st indicates strength of the reversal. If the 3rd candle (green) is bigger than 1st candle (red), the greater is the strength of reversal. The bulls finally take the control &

start buying. The stock price will move upward. You can initiate a bullish option strategy like buying of Calls, selling of Puts, Buying Covered Call, Bull Call Spread, Bull Put Spread etc. just above the high of the Doji line after confirmation of Morning Star signal with rising volume. Prices should cross above the level of last closing price for confirmation. The bottom of the Doji is a good support line and stop loss may be placed at or just below the bottom line.

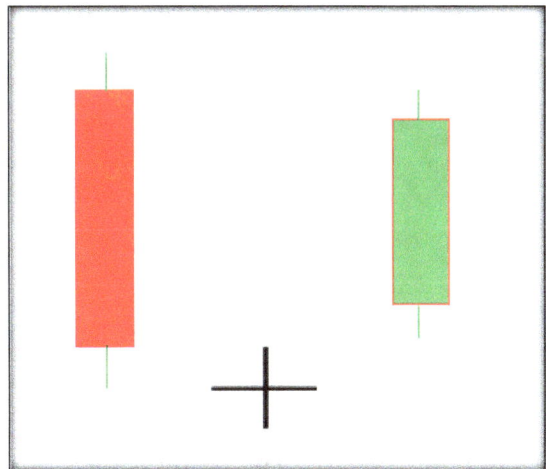

The emergence of Morning Star candle in the downtrend gives bullish reversal signal. The stock price increases with successive long green candles. The traders who have sold into a market might consider this as a signal to start looking to exit their respective short trades and find opportunity to buy.

Bullish Harami:- In a down trend, when a smaller white or green candle completely engulfed by the previous day larger black or red candle; Bullish Harami signal is formed. As soon as the bullish harami got confirmed, there is possibility of trend reversal. The bulls finally take the control & start buying. The stock price will move upward. You can initiate a bullish option strategy like buying of Calls, selling of Puts, Buying Covered Call, Bull Call Spread, Bull Put Spread etc. upon confirmation of Bullish Harami signal with rising volume. For confirmation, Prices should cross above the last close or the midpoint of the 1st Red body, whichever is higher. The bottom of the bullish candle is a good support line and **Stop Loss** is placed at or just below the bottom line.

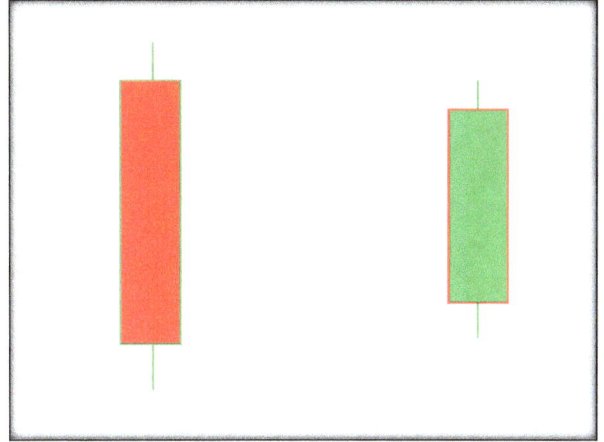

Three White Soldiers Pattern:- Consists of three consecutive bullish candles at the end of a bearish trend. Each one opens within the previous candle's real body and closes higher than the previous candle. This pattern indicates weakness in the ongoing downtrend and signals future uptrend. Also, such pattern indicates shifting of control from bears to the bulls & prospective trend reversal.

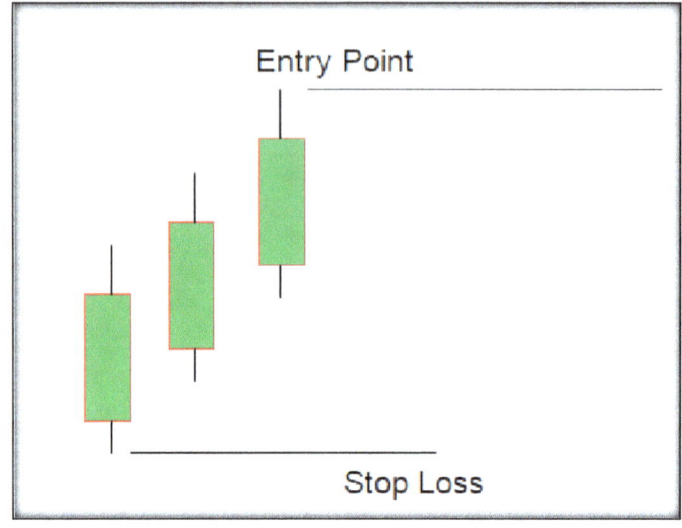

Bullish Engulfing:- In a down trend, when a larger white or green candle completely engulfs the previous day smaller black or red candle; Bullish Engulfing signal is formed. This generates a bullish signal if occurs in oversold conditions and bearish signal if occurs in overbought conditions. The stock price closes above the open of the previous day. Smart & Big money starts buying. After confirmation of continued buying, there is possibility of trend reversal. The bulls finally take the control & start buying. The stock price will move upward. The bottom of the bullish candle is a good support line and **Stop Loss** is placed at or just below the line. You can initiate a bullish option strategy like buying of Calls, selling of Puts, Buying Covered Call, Bull Call Spread, Bull Put Spread etc. upon confirmation of Bullish Engulfing signal with rising volume. Prices should cross above the level of last closing price for confirmation.

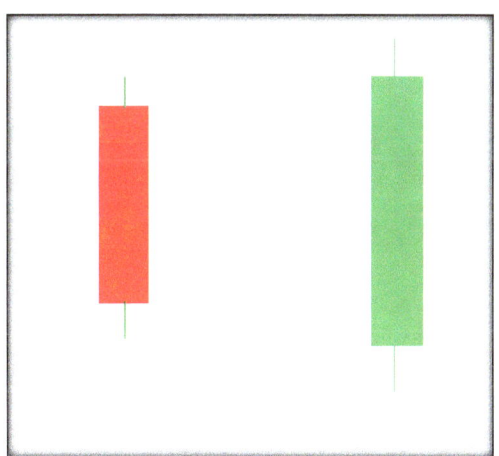

Bullish Abandon Baby:- Abandoned Baby, a rare formation reversal pattern made up three candles appears in both uptrend & down trend and is more decisive than Doji candle. It is similar to the Morning &

Evening Star formations. Bullish abandon baby is formed following a down trend.

The first candle is long body, bearish in nature. The second candle is doji formed gapped down from 1st candle and third candle is long body, strong bullish in nature formed gap up from 2nd candle and closes above 50% of 1st candle.

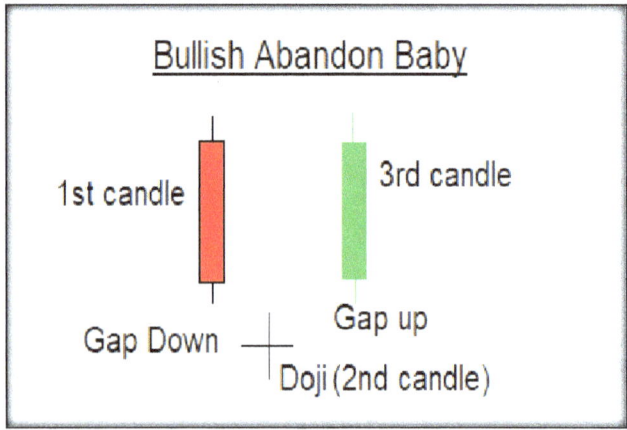

Falling Wedge Pattern:- Wedge pattern is a reversal pattern. Rising wedge accompanied with bearish breakout and falling wedge with bullish breakout.

Falling Wedge is a chart pattern, which formed when the price action makes lower highs & lower lows in contracting sequences. The subsequent highs & lows are defiantly lower than the previous high & low. It is also a fact that, the volume decreases as the price action progresses. The upper line is considered as resistance and lower line is considered as support. These two converging lines must have been touched twice to be considered as wedge pattern.

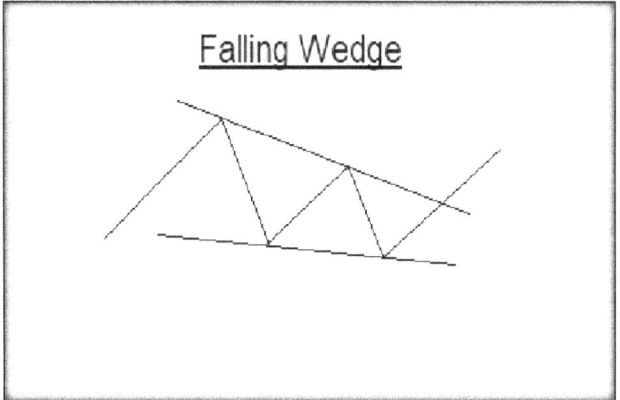

Falling Wedge

Bullish Pin Bar:- Pin Bar is powerful pattern of price reversal. It has a small body & long tail distinctly visible. Depending upon the colour of the small body and position of long tail, it is described as Bullish Pin

Bar & Bearish Pin Bar. Bullish Pin Bar is having small green body at top with little or no wick at the top and long wick at the bottom. A bullish Pin Bar appears at the end of the down trend. The pattern must be confirmed by the bullish candlestick that opens above the closing price of the Pin Bar. The tail of the Pin Bar shows rejection of price and ensuing reversal.

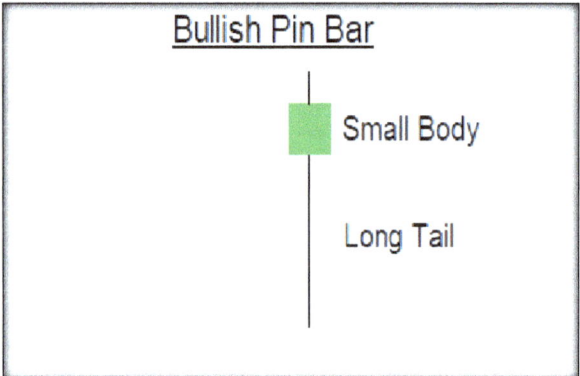

Piercing Candlestick Pattern:- A Piercing candlestick pattern is a bullish reversal pattern, that happen usually in down trend. On the way to down trend, when one long bearish candle appears followed by one relatively smaller size bullish candle, which closes above 50% of the preceding bearish candle; such piercing candlestick pattern happens.

The piercing pattern involves two candlesticks, the second bullish one is opening gap down below the closing price of first bearish candle. The closing price of 2nd bullish candle is above 50% line of the 1st candle. This pattern implicates, the market begins with a bearish impulse, but eventually, bulls enter the market and push prices higher. Buyers gained momentum to drag the market up, thus, trend reversal.

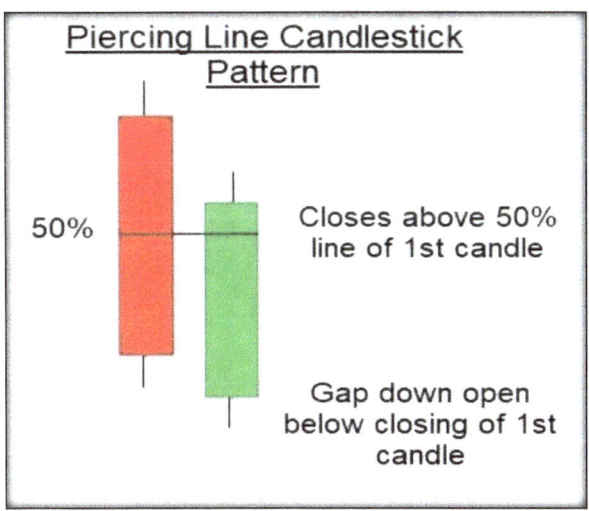

BEARISH REVERSAL PATTERNS

For Bearish Divergence, traders would analyze at the highs on the indicator & price action. If the price exhibits higher highs but the indicator exhibits lower highs, it is construed as bearish divergence. This may indicate price action with strong selling pressure with appearance of divergence. In uptrend, when price pattern appears as double top, triple top, head & shoulder and special candle like hanging man, shooting star & evening star etc., the price action might take reversal and move down ward. These are called as bearish reversal pattern. Some of the bearish reversal patterns are as depicted below.

Double Top:- A double top is a price pattern in stock chart, resembling the English letter 'M' & signal for a bearish price movement. A short position is initiated with downside breakout. Stop Loss is placed just above the break down point or at the second top of the pattern. The profit target would be the height of the pattern. The traders or investors initiate bearish strategy upon emergence of double top pattern.

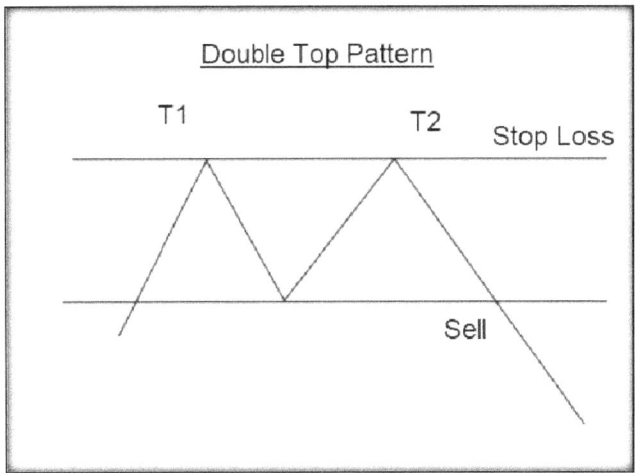

The more wider gaps between the touches in double top pattern, the more powerful the pattern becomes. It is often found that, double bottom is somewhat more effective pattern in breakout strategy.

Triple Top:- The triple top is a bearish reversal pattern that occurs at the end of an uptrend. The triple top consists of the three consecutive highs at the same or near same level. A short position is initiated with downside break down. Stop Loss is placed just above the break down point or at the 3rd top of the pattern.

The profit target would be the height of the pattern. The traders or investors initiate bearish strategy upon emergence of tripple top pattern.

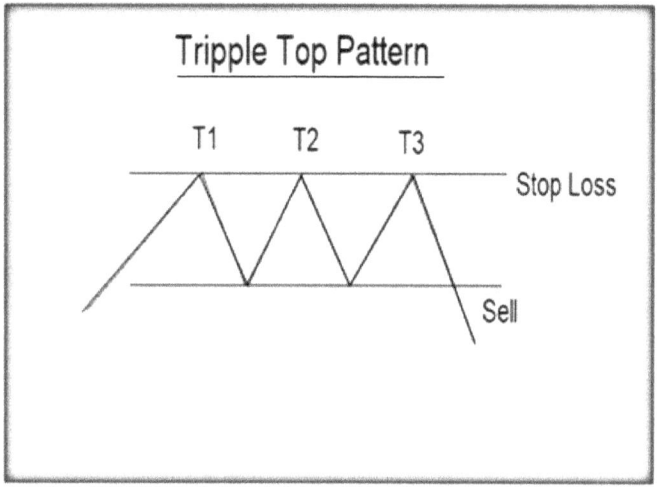

Head & Shoulder:- Head & Shoulder is a bearish reversal pattern which is formed during an uptrend. It has three successive peaks; the middle peak (head) being the highest and two lower side peaks of nearly equal height (left & right shoulders). The base line is called neckline. The volume of buying decreases from left peak (left shoulder) to right peak (right shoulder) through middle peak (head). Due to downward trend of prices from the right shoulder, focus of the traders are shifted from buying to selling. The most common entry point is the breakdown from the neckline. The height of the pattern from the breakdown price will be the profit target. Stop Loss will be placed at the peak of right shoulder above neck line.

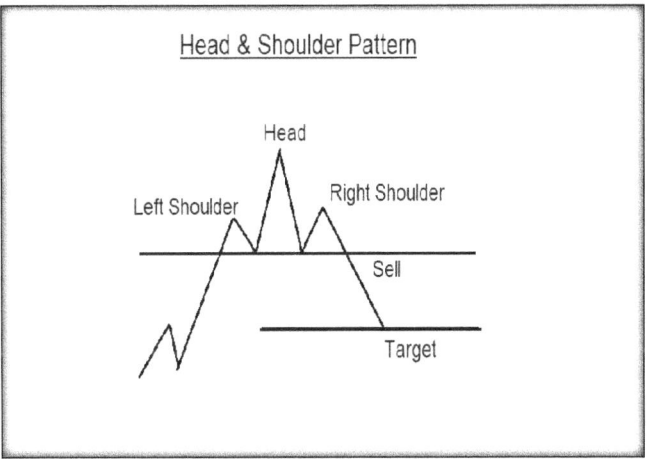

Hanging Man:- A small green or red candle body having long lower shadow with or without small upper shadow found during an uptrend. Both Hanging Man & Hammer looks exactly same in appearance; but the former forms in an uptrend and the later form in a downtrend. Irrespective of the colour of the body, hanging man indicates a bearish signal. Red hanging man is more bearish than a Green hanging man. With the formation of Hanging Man, the Bears finally take the control & start selling. Thus, hanging man is a bearish reversal pattern. The top of the Hanging Man signal is the resistance line and stop loss may be placed at or just above the top line.

The emergence of Hanging Man candle in the uptrend gives bearish reversal signal. When one hanging man candle appears, the stock price takes reversal and plunges downward. The traders who have bought into a market might consider this as a signal to start looking to exit their respective long trades and find opportunities to short sell.

Shooting Star:- A small green or red candlestick body having long upper shadow with little or no lower shadow; found during an uptrend. Basically a Shooting Star is a Hanging Man flipped upside down. Irrespective of the colour of the body, shooting star indicates a bearish reversal signal. Red body is more bearish than a green body. With the formation of Shooting Star, the bears finally take the control & start selling. Prices should cross below the low of the Inverted Hammer's body for sell confirmation. The top of the Shooting Star is the resistance line and stop loss may be placed at or just above the upper wick. Shooting star & Inverted hammer looks alike. But the former forms in an uptrend and the later forms in a down trend. Hence Shooting star is bearish reversal pattern and inverted hammer is bullish reversal pattern.

When shooting star pattern appears, the stock price takes reversal and plunges downward. The traders who have bought into a market might consider this as a signal to start looking to exit their respective

long trades and find opportunities to short sell.

Evening Star:- Evening Star pattern is a

combination of 3 candles. When a large green candle

followed by Doji and a smaller red candle found in an

uptrend, an Evening Star signal is formed. The 1st

candle is green, the 2nd candle formed gap up or

normal and may be of any colour, but either doji or

spinning top and the 3rd candle formed gap down or

normal and red in colour. Evening Star indicates

something bad to come i.e., the stock price/index will

decline. As soon as the Evening Star pattern is

confirmed, there is possibility of trend reversal. If the 3rd

candle (red) is bigger than 1st candle (green), the

greater is the strength of reversal. The bears finally take the control & start selling. The stock price will move downward. The traders can initiate a bearish option strategy like buying of Puts, selling of Calls, Bear Put Spread, Bear Call spread etc. just below the low of the Doji line after confirmation of Evening Star signal with rising volume. The top of the Doji is a good resistance line and stop loss may be placed at or just above the top line.

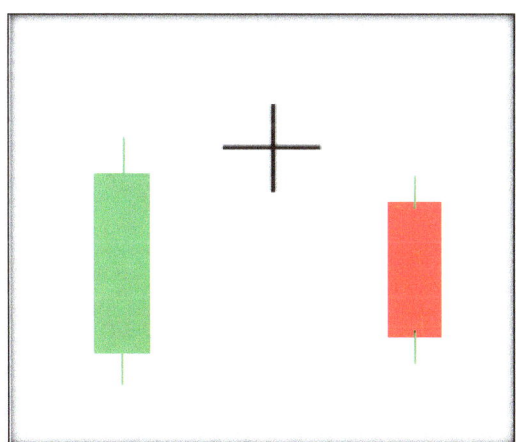

Upon emergence of Evening Star pattern, the stock price decreases with successive long red candles. The traders who have bought into a market might consider this as a signal to start looking to exit their respective long trades and find opportunities to short sell.

Bearish Harami:- In an uptrend, when a smaller black or red candle completely engulfed by the previous day larger white or green candle; Bearish Harami signal is formed. As soon as the bearish harami got confirmed, there is possibility of trend reversal. The bears finally take the control & start selling. The stock price will move downward. You can initiate a bearish option strategy like buying of Puts, selling of Calls, Bear Put Spread, Bear Call spread etc. after confirmation of Bearish Harami signal with rising volume. For confirmation, Prices should cross below the last close or the midpoint of the 1st Green body, whichever is lower. The top of the bearish candle is the resistance line and **Stop Loss** is placed at or just above the top line.

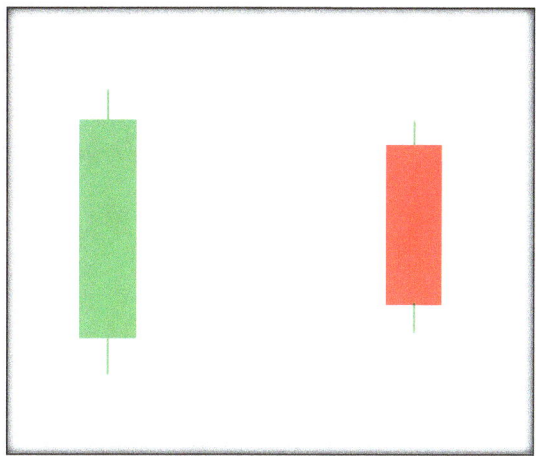

Three Black Crows Pattern:- Consists of three consecutive bearish candles at the end of a bullish trend. In this pattern, each one is opening below the previous one and closes lower than the previous candle. This indicates weakness in the ongoing uptrend and signals future down trend. Such pattern indicates shifting of control from bulls to the bears & prospective trend reversal.

The opposite of three black crows pattern is three white soldiers pattern. Three successive red candles in uptrend indicate the bears are now ready to push the prices downward.

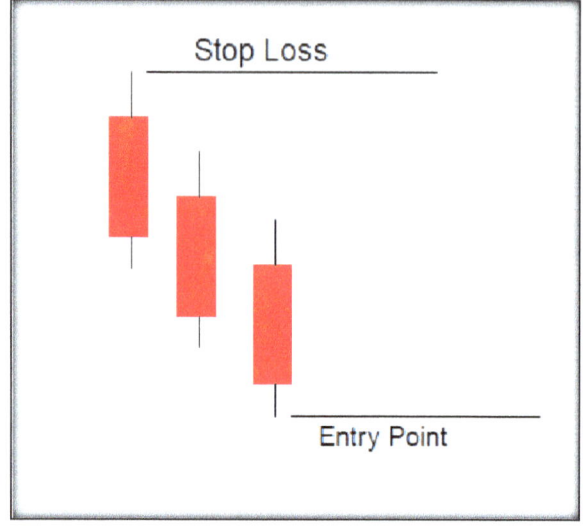

Bearish Engulfing:- In an uptrend, when a larger black or red candle completely engulfs the previous day smaller white or green candle; Bearish Engulfing signal is formed. This generates a bearish signal if occurs in overbought conditions and bullish signal if occurs in oversold conditions. The stock price closes below the open of the previous day. Smart & Big money starts selling. There is possibility of trend reversal. Prices should cross below the last closing price for sell confirmation. The bears finally take the control & start selling. The stock price will move downward. The top of the bearish candle is the resistance line and **Stop Loss** is placed at or just above the line.

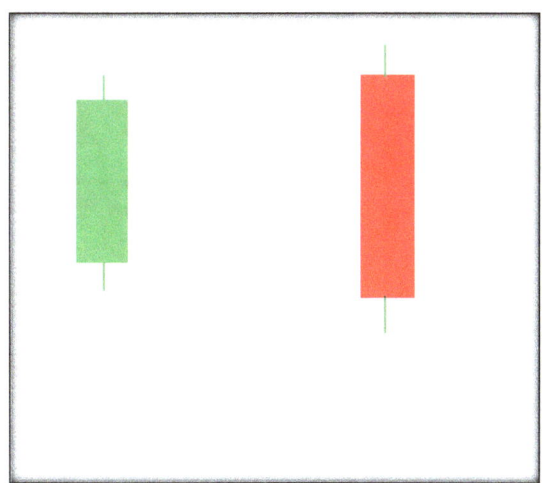

Bearish Abandon Baby:- Bearish abandon baby is bearish reversal pattern formed following an uptrend. The first candle is long body, bullish in nature. The second candle is doji formed gapped up from 1st candle and third candle is long body, strong bearish in nature and formed gap down from 2nd candle and closes below 50% of 1st candle.

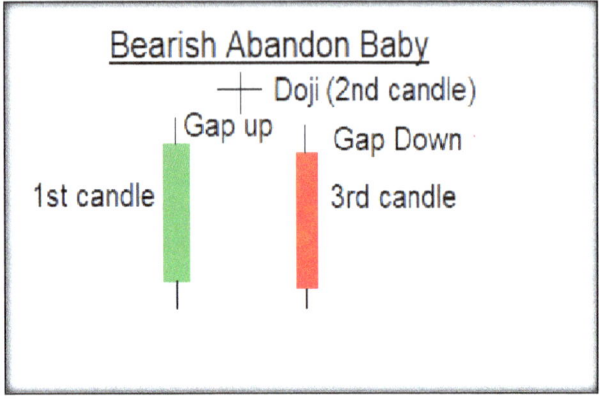

In this case, initially the bulls had control and pushed the prices higher. However later on, the bears were able to gain control and push the prices down.

Dark Cloud Cover:- Dark Cloud Cover is a bearish reversal candlestick pattern. It usually occurs in an uptrend near resistance level. The first candle is bullish and long body. The second candle is bearish and also long body, significantly open above the 1st candle (gap up opening) and closes below 50% of 1st candle. It means, candle opens higher than previous day close price and closes below midpoint previous day candle.

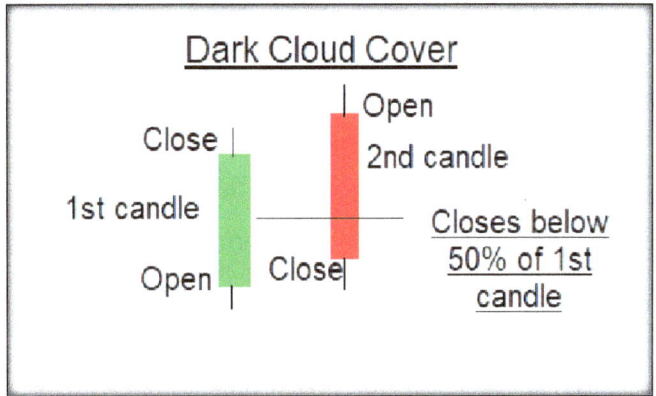

The rejection of the gap up hold on to a bearish sign and bulls are unable to maintain the prices higher. A small red candle next to the dark cloud cover pattern indicates confirmation. Traders exit the long position and initiate short position. The dark cloud cover pattern is the opposite of Piercing Pattern. Piercing pattern occurs at the end of a down trend, where as dark cloud cover occurs at the end of an uptrend.

Rising Wedge:- A wedge is a price pattern characterized by converging trend lines on a stock price chart. Wedge patterns have tendency to break in the opposite direction from the prevailing trend line. Rising Wedge pattern signals a bearish reversal pattern.

Rising Wedge often happens in uptrend. Stock price advances upward in higher high & higher low trend. Buying pressure gradually decreases due to the fact that, stock price refuses to break the upper level of resistance. Subsequently, the lower level of support is broken and price breaks down, begins a strong down trend.

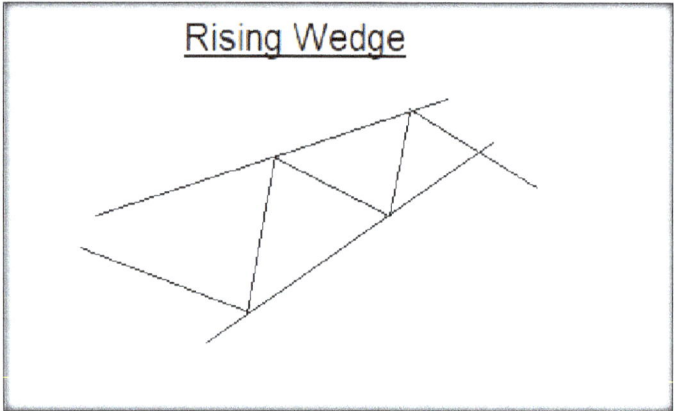

Bearish Pin Bar:- Pin Bar is powerful pattern of price reversal. It has a small body & long tail distinctly visible. Bearish Pin Bar is having small red body at the bottom with little or no wick at the bottom and long wick at the top. A bearish Pin Bar appears at the end of the uptrend. The pattern must be confirmed by the bearish candlestick that opens below the closing price of the Pin Bar.

TREND REVERSAL

In Stock market investing, for every winner there is one looser on the other side of the game. With every trade there is someone who wants to buy and someone who wants to sell the stock. The buyer groups are called Bulls and the seller groups are called Bears. The stock market struggles between the Bulls & the Bears. Bull pushes the market up and bear pushes the market down. If bulls are stronger, sentiment is positive. If bears are stronger, sentiment is negative. If both are uniform, sentiment is neutral. The successful investors/traders extract information from the market to find out the dominant groups and move with them.

Reversal pattern is formation of candlesticks which indicate the culmination of prevailing trend; and move either up or down. At the beginning of a reversal, it is not clear whether it is a reversal or a minor pull back. Stock prices tend to test multiple upside and downside reversal over time. A trend reversal marks the end of an existing trend and beginning of a new trend. Such reversal may happen in any time frame.

Correction or minor pull back happens very often and does not depend on fundamental factors. Conversely, reversal is most often preceded by event-filled news release. Reversal can happen at any time, characterized by change in the overall trend of price action. Reversal typically characterized by large price changes in opposite direction. Uptrend reverses in to down trend and down trend reverses in to uptrend. In uptrend with falling prices and in down trend with rising prices.

The overall direction of price action is called trend. The overall trend does not change abruptly. The prices of stocks usually fluctuate in zig zag fashion and often follow a general trend, either up or down. The zig zag movement of price action creates minor pull back, correction or retracement, which are synonymous with each other and does not affect the overall trend of the market. Stock prices usually go up steadily in a flatter slope. Conversely, stock prices fall down abruptly in a steep slope. In uptrend, traders look at the lower support points and anticipate it to break. In down trend, traders look at the higher resistance points and anticipate it to break. Such upward or downward trends may last for months or even years, depending upon the demand & supply factor. When demand for a particular stock or index changes, the prevailing trend reverses and price action begins to move in opposite direction. The buying & selling pressure altered and traders have to take appropriate decisions.

When the bullish candles are getting larger, it is implied that buying pressure is getting stronger and uptrend is ensuing. When the bearish candles are getting larger, it is implied that selling pressure is getting stronger and down trend is ensuing.

When the bullish candles are getting smaller, it is implied that buying pressure is weakening and bullish momentum is decreasing. When the bearish candles are getting smaller, it is implied that selling pressure is weakening and bearish momentum is decreasing.

It is depicted that, if the stock or index price is above the moving average, it indicates uptrend and if the stock or index price is below the moving average, it indicates down trend. The direction of the moving average indicates the prevailing market trend. Upward moving average contemplates uptrend and down ward moving average contemplates down trend. A change in the slope of the moving average also indicate a change in trend. In uptrend, the reversal will be confirmed when the price action crosses below the moving average. In down trend, the reversal will be confirmed when the price action crosses above the moving average.

When price action is analyzed in conjunction with Bollinger Band, price reversal is anticipated when price action moves below the middle line. Trend reversal in

MACD happens when, MACD line & signal line make crossover.

When the market dwells in the upper level, signify that the stock has been bought more than the expectation of the market and considered overbought. Conversely, when the market dwells in the lower level, signify that the stock has been sold more than the expectation of the market and considered oversold. In the oversold zone, the stock prices might be reversed and take u-turn to move upward. In the overbought zone, the stock prices might be reversed and take u-turn to move down ward.

STRATEGY DISCUSSION FOR DIVERGENCE & PRICE ACTION

Human nature diehard. People commit the same mistakes time & again. The repetition of human memories motivate to repeat the history itself. Due to the repetitive nature of market participants and reaction to global news, the price action of stock or index also tends to repeat itself in various patterns. Technical analysis study the effects of price patterns. The repetition of history (past pattern) is the basis of technical analysis. Technical analysis is a derivative of price action. Short term traders & investors exclusively rely on price action.

There are several techniques that traders can use to make entry & exit strategy to enhance the chances of success & minimize potential losses. Some of the techniques are trend lines and Support & Resistance levels. Trend line identify the direction of the trend and when to enter & exit the trade. Support &

Resistance identify the critical levels at which the price is likely to reverse or continue its trend.

Price Action analysis is based on the assumption that, stock prices exhibit all vital information and looking at how prices moved in the past can predict how prices will be moved in future. Price Action is an approach to interpret market sentiments and the driving forces for the price action. Trend Lines, Support & Resistance and Candlestick Patterns are used to decide entry & exit points.

Price Action is generated by any inventory that is bought or sold in a financial market. Thus, Price Action is influenced by the sentiments of market participants. Price action traders make use of past history of market price movements, which include swing highs & swing lows and support & resistance levels as well. They interpret the price action and predict the next move for the security in stock market.

For Price Action trading, Candlestick chart is ordinarily accepted as the best type of chart to be used. Price Action trading is most suitable for short to medium term instead of long term investment.

Price Action manifested the premise for all technical analysis interpretations. All the technical tools & indicators are built over the basic data from price action. Thus, technical analysis is considered as derivative of price action. Support & Resistance, different candlestick patterns and trend lines are used to take trading decisions. Inspite of veracity of price action, when it is analyzed by different traders; one trader may see a bullish sentiment and another might be anticipate trend reversal if pursued divergence.

Most of the time, if the price action is making higher highs, the indicator should also follow by making higher highs. If price action advances with lower lows, indicator also moves with lower lows. If not, price action & indicator are diverging from each other. It is also

79

found that, divergence is not found in all price reversals. Hence, Divergence could be a valuable addition to the existing strategy. If the price action analysis tells, the price is about to rise, the traders want to initiate a long position. If they believe the price will fall, the traders may want to initiate a short position. The slope of the divergence depicts the momentum of the trend reversal. Bigger the slope, higher the chances of occurrence of price reversal.

Divergence occurs usually after every big move. But, most big moves are not immediately associated with reversal. Hence confirmation of price action is essential using other indicators. Divergence helps out to visualize a possible trend reversal ahead of time to decide exit or entry points. All Profits & Losses in stock market trading are based on price. Divergences on shorter time frames occur more frequently but are less reliable than divergences on longer timeframes.

Divergence works on all indicators, but commonly used indicators include Relative Strength Index, Stochastic, Moving Average Convergence Divergence (MACD) etc. Bullish divergence depicts, bears are loosing power and bulls are ready to control the market again. Often, bullish divergence marks the end of downtrend. When one divergence is established, but the price has already moved out for some reason, the divergence should be considered played out.

Divergence is a concept, rarely visible in technical analysis. If you follow only price action, you can see uptrend, down trend & sideways trend. Divergence is seen with certain oscillators like RSI, Stochastics & MACD etc. Without indicator, no divergence is visualized. Thus, divergence is hidden in the price action, which is identified by the experienced traders with the help of indicator. Indicator, when advances opposite to the price action create divergence. Bullish divergence often happens in down trend and traders usually connect lows on price action and lows on the indicator as well to visualize the discrepancy between them. Bearish divergence often happens in uptrend and traders usually connect highs on price action and highs on the indicator as well to visualize the discrepancy between them.

It is imperative to wait for the confirmation candle after divergence. If the candle closes differently, the trading signal from divergence can pass from sight as swiftly as it took shape. Use other indicators to confirm the signal.

Even if the divergence occurs, there is no guarantee that price will reverse any time soon. Hence, when a reversal candle appears, the traders need to consider the strength of the signal. If reversal candle is confirmed, three options come out before the traders.

i.   If signal is strong, existing traders exit all of the positions.

ii.   If signal is not so strong, existing traders tighten the stop loss and close out part position.

iii.   New traders initiate new positions in the direction of reversal.

Sometimes, the divergence may give false signals and the stock price moves as earlier, without changing the trend. However, the major advantage of using divergence is that, it gives trading signal well before the price action has changed. Such early signal provides the traders better entry & exit price and also placing stop loss.

Bearish reversal pattern indicates that the sellers have taken over the buyers. Conversely, Bullish reversal pattern indicates that the buyers have taken over the sellers. When a bullish reversal is seen, stop loss is placed below the entire pattern's low. Conversely, when a bearish reversal is seen, stop loss is placed above the entire pattern's high. After confirmation of reversal candle, trade entry, tightening stop loss & taking away profit is suitably decided.

Pullback or Correction is temporary and lasts for a few trading sessions, while reversal signify complete change in market sentiment. Uptrend switched to downtrend or vice versa.

The high hit by a stock is called peak and lows of a stock are called troughs. The up trending stocks consistently hit high peaks & high troughs. The down trending stocks consistently hit low peaks & low troughs. When the stock price makes flat peaks & flat troughs, the trend is considered as sideways trend.

Trend Lines are typically drawn along rising swing lows during an uptrend and falling swing highs during a downtrend. Thus, uptrend lines have positive slope and is formed by connecting at least three low points. Similarly, the down trend lines have negative slope and is formed by connecting at least three high points.

Large body Candles with small wicks indicate strong momentum, while small body candles with large wicks indicate indecision. When the bearish candles are getting larger, it tells you the selling pressure is getting stronger as the buyers are unwilling to buy at such prices. Conversely, when the bullish candles are getting larger, it tells you the buying pressure is getting stronger as the sellers are unwilling to sell at such prices.

Stock market tends to more volatile at certain times of the day and tends to less volatile at other times. Usually, trading session starts and ends with high volatility, characterized by long range bars. At the middle of each session, the market might be less volatile, characterized by narrow range bars.

The price action of the stock market is driven by some emotional forces like demand & supply and emotions of market participants. When the crowd sentiment is strong, sometimes, divergence may not provide actual result. Hence divergence may be visualized carefully.

Indicators work on price data and usually follow a price action. Sometimes, indicator does not follow price path and shows divergence from price action. Just opposite of price action to signal reversal or exhaustion of price action beforehand. This discrepancy of price action and indicator facilitates the traders to take appropriate action well before the trend change. Price action is analyzed to take short term trade, while indicator is used to take medium to long term.

WEBSITES MAY BE SEEN

google.com

investing.com

tradingview.com

nseindia.com

bseindia.com

moneycontrol.com

rediffmoney.com

icicidirect.com

elearnmarkets.com

chartink.com

BOOKS MAY BE READ

1. Intelligent Investor — Benjamin Graham
2. Common Stocks & Uncommon Profits — Philip A. Fisher
3. Options made easy — Guy Cohen
4. Learn to Earn — Peter Lynch
5. One up on Wall Street — Peter Lynch
6. Beating the Street — Peter Lynch
7. Business Adventure — John Brooks
8. Random Walk Down Wall Street — Burton G. Malkeil
9. Rule No. 1 — Phil Town
10. Stocks for the Long Run — Jeremy J. Siegel
11. Where are the Customers' Yachts? — Fred Schwed
12. How I Made $ 2000000 in the Stock Market — Nicolas Darvas
13. Trading for a Living — Dr. Alexander Elder
14. Momentum Explained — Martin J. Pring
15. Irrational Exuberance — Robert J. Shiller
16. Mastering the Trade — John F. Carter
17. Trend Following — Michael Covel
18. The New Market Wizard — Jack D. Schwager

ABOUT THE AUTHOR

Er. Sudhir Kumar Sahu was born to Sj. Sarat Kumar Sahu & Smt. Jagyanseni Sahu on 9th October 1965. Now he is working as Superintending Engineer, Main Dam Division, Burla. Joined in the department of Water Resources, Govt. of Odisha as Assistant Engineer way back in 1994 and worked in different irrigation projects in different capacity. He has been associated with 14 professional bodies and associations pertaining to engineering organizations. He is also a fellow of the Indian Water Resources Society & Indian Association of Hydrologists.

He has published 11 books namely "The Portfolio of Mythological Events", "The Portfolio of National & International Events", "The Kernel of Stock Market Investing", "The Compilation of Options Strategy" , "The Precept of Stop Loss", "The Paradox of Put Call Ratio", "Iron Condor & Reverse Iron Condor", "Iron Butterfly & Reverse Iron Butterfly", "Ichimoku Clouds", "Heiken Ashi Candles", "Dollar Cost Averaging & Covered Call Strategy" etc. in Amazon.com. This is his 12th book. His better half Smt. Sasmita Sahoo, P.G. Diploma in Nutrition & Dietetics and home makers; having been blessed with two daughters; Samanwita & Samapika. Samanwita Pursued B.Tech. (Comp. Sc.) & working as module lead in LTIMindtree Ltd. and Samapika studying BA in Delhi University, a Civil Service aspirant.

www.ingramcontent.com/pod-product-compliance
Lightning Source LLC
Chambersburg PA
CBHW070436220526
45466CB00004B/1706